Contempo (1929): "Air Conquest. Icarus' wings have melted, like a blazing star he falls to earth."

John VASSOS

CONTEMPO, PHOBIA AND OTHER GRAPHIC INTERPRETATIONS

With a Foreword by P. K. THOMAJAN

DOVER PUBLICATIONS, INC., NEW YORK

DEDICATED TO THE BRILLIANT POLYMORPHIC MEMORY OF
HARRY STACK SULLIVAN

Published in Canada by General Publishing Company, Ltd., 30 Lesmill Road, Don Mills, Toronto, Ontario.
Published in the United Kingdom by Constable and Company, Ltd., 10 Orange Street, London WC 2.

Contempo, Phobia and Other Graphic Interpretations by John Vassos is a new work, first published by Dover Publications, Inc., in 1976.

International Standard Book Number: 0-486-23338-3
Library of Congress Catalog Card Number: 76-696

Manufactured in the United States of America
Dover Publications, Inc.
180 Varick Street
New York, N.Y. 10014

ARTIST'S ACKNOWLEDGMENT

It was gracious of John Mayfield and the University of Syracuse Library to lend us 33 illustrations from the Mayfield Collection, including the 23 from my book *Phobia*.

Phobia has been out of print for many years and is now a collector's item. The original book was dedicated to my friend Harry Stack Sullivan, the eminent psychiatrist. He guided me to the realization of *Phobia* and had a profound influence on my life.

The lengthy introduction with detailed explanations in the original volume are not included in the Dover edition (nor are the full texts of my other books). However, a brief identification of each phobia (and brief textual extracts from the other books) will help the reader to understand the meaning behind the pictures. There are three drives that are evident in phobias: the will to power, sex gratification and the desire for suicide. In this volume, as in the original, the phobias are arranged in order of progressive intensity.

I also take this opportunity to thank my other friends who came forth with originals from their collections to make this anthology of my work possible.

JOHN VASSOS

The publisher, as well as the artist, is most grateful to the following lenders of original gouaches:

The Mayfield Library of Manuscripts and Rare Books at Syracuse University: Plates 49 through 79 and Plate 103.
Mr. Albert Baer (N.Y.): Plate 19.
Mrs. Ellie T. Brohl (Blackwood, N.J.): Plate 43.
Mr. Robert K. Brown (N.Y.): Plates 3, 31, 35 and 48.
Mr. and Mrs. Hayward Cirker (N.Y.): Plate 39.
Ms. Margarette Cruz (N.Y.): Plate 28.
Mrs. Frances P. Johnes (Levittown, N.Y.): Plate 26.
Mr. and Mrs. Robert Kerdasha (N.Y.): Plates 29 and 38.
Ms. Marthe Krueger (Wilton, Conn.): Plates 25 and 106.
Mr. Edmond Lilly (N.Y.): Plate 102.
Mr. P. K. Thomajan (Carlstadt, N.J.): Plate 4.

The original gouaches for all the other plates are from the collection of the artist.

PUBLISHER'S NOTE

All the plates in this collection have been reproduced directly from the original black-and-white gouaches by John Vassos. Most of them were created as illustrations for the following nine books:

Salomé, A Tragedy in One Act by Oscar Wilde, Inventions by John Vassos, 1927.

The Ballad of Reading Gaol by Oscar Wilde, Conceptions by John Vassos, 1928 (edition limited to 200 copies).

The Harlot's House and Other Poems by Oscar Wilde, Interpretations by John Vassos, 1929.

Contempo; This American Tempo, Creations by John Vassos, Text by Ruth Vassos, 1929.

Ultimo; An Imaginative Narration of Life Under the Earth with Projections by John Vassos and the Text by Ruth Vassos, 1930.

Elegy in a Country Church-Yard Written by Thomas Gray and Newly Created into an Illustrated Book by John Vassos [*Gray's Elegy*], 1931.

Phobia by John Vassos, 1931 (edition limited to 1500 copies).

Kubla Khan, Samuel Coleridge's Poem with Interpretive Illustrations by John Vassos, 1933.

Humanities, John Vassos Illustrates—with the Text by Ruth Vassos, 1935 (edition limited to 2000 copies).

With the exception of *Phobia* (Covici, Friede, N.Y.), all of these were published by E. P. Dutton and Co., Inc., N.Y.

Vassos' books were typical of a significant publishing trend of the Twenties and early Thirties: the expensive illustrated limited edition. The luxury volumes of these years contain the finest American examples of Art Deco illustration; in company with Rockwell Kent and Lynd Ward, Vassos is the outstanding figure in this area. In fact, his dazzling hard-line gouaches in black, white and subtly controlled tones of gray are even more distinctively Art Deco than the more traditional woodcut or pen techniques of the other two masters.

Like Kent and Ward, Vassos retained his faith in the human figure at a time when abstraction was making great inroads; and, like them, he had the power to create satisfying total compositions based on his simplified forms. But perhaps the most important feature these three artists had in common was their humanistic message, their use of Art Deco not merely to provide superficial ornament, attractive as that might be, but also (like the Mexican muralists) to grapple with big social and political themes and participate in the major intellectual currents of their time. Mr. P. K. Thomajan's highly personal and encomiastic Foreword delves thoroughly into the details of Vassos' contributions in this respect.

Thanks to our good fortune in obtaining Vassos' original gouaches, and thanks to the enormous strides that offset lithography has made since the Thirties, the reproductions in the present volume are far superior to those in the first editions of the Vassos books. A very few of these original gouaches have become slightly discolored in the course of time (never enough to prevent full enjoyment of the art); we have decided to include these in order to present Vassos in all his variety.

FOREWORD
by P. K. Thomajan

In the annals of American art, John Vassos stands out in a genre all his own, that of a mystic-realist, a rare blend of the subjective and the objective. He belongs to no school, has no cult.

Citations and awards have accrued to Vassos in the course of his long career, recognition for accomplishments in various areas of activity. There have been exhibitions and testimonial dinners in his honor, while his originals command increasing attention and prices at galleries and auction rooms. His works are to be found in the permanent collections of museums and universities, evidence that this Renaissance man ranks as a legend in his time.

Many critics were prompt to recognize this newcomer in the realm of art, saluted his visual innovations. Art Young remarked, "Vassos saves modern art from dementia praecox."

Among the various artists of the past, Vassos finds a few affinities: Daumier for his satiric castigations, Van Gogh for his bold break with tradition, Blake for his cosmic imagination, Doré for his climactic vistas.

Exposure to his images has proven of psychiatric value, a source of subliminal satisfactions and psychic release. Out of the folds of his fluent figures many discern truths and prophetic visions.

Time and again, Vassos subtly shuffles esoteric traceries into his compositions, such as Yang and Yin in *Salomé,* which imparted a sexual leaven. Vassos is at his best when dreaming up *phantomotifs* in the twilight zone of consciousness. He scrutinizes the inscrutable, extroverts and surfaces submerged meanings. Even his symbolic abstractions, that may appear to float in space, possess a relevant reality and precise fitment into his scheme of things.

As a rule, image concepts come to the artist's mind with a complete totality. Thus, conception and execution are more or less simultaneous, which makes for spontaneity. Usually he makes small pencil sketches as preliminaries. These are rarely altered when he swings into the finish. Remarks Vassos, "I find that my mind works with the precision of a computer once I have subconsciously assimilated and programmed a project."

Vassos considers himself fortunate in having connected with two kinetic entities in his lifetime. First and foremost was his wife, the former Ruth Carriere, whom he met at a Greenwich Village soirée in 1924. She was a fashion adviser to Saks-Fifth Avenue and had the gift of words. Together, they made a visual/verbal team that produced several of the books represented here. The second decisive acquaintance was that of the eminent psychiatrist Harry Stack Sullivan, regarded as the Freud of America, to whom *Phobia* is dedicated.

Visual literacy, an uncommon trait, is a key Vassos asset. It enables him to articulate images that assume a dominant role in his books. In fact, his effects often establish new dimensions of meaning. In the Gray, Wilde and Coleridge books, he achieves touches that the authors could never approximate via the medium of words.

Vassos veers away from the word "illustration," which appears only in the full titles of the Gray, Coleridge and *Humanities.* To him, it is trite and limited. He prefers to call his images "creations," "inventions," "interpretations," "conceptions." These terms convey more scope and breadth.

Now and then, Vassos will confess that he feels like a frustrated movie director. One year that he happened to skip without producing a book, any number of Hollywood devotees wrote him, remarking, "How can we make new pictures when Vassos does not give us the inspiration?" Vassos' compositions have a definite cinematic quality: they are multidimensional, with fade-ins, fade-outs, close-ups, long shots, lap dissolves. His complex vision achieves graphic montages of the visual elements, and his silhouette effects capture a moment of pantomime.

Vassos may be numbered among the tradition-shattering personalities who thrived in the spectacular 1920's, when the arts cut loose from the apron strings of binding traditions. The younger generation, disillusioned by World War I, emerged from its age of innocence, questioned leaders and institutions, toppled old idols, crusaded against injustices. The Vassos books, especially *Ultimo, Humanities* and *Contempo,* made powerful visual indictments.

Vassos' books fall into two categories: those composed around classic authors (Gray's *Elegy in a Country Church-Yard,* Coleridge's *Kubla Khan,* Oscar Wilde's *Salomé, Harlot's House* and *Ballad of Reading Gaol)* and the originals *(Contempo, Ultimo* and *Humanities* with text by Ruth Vassos, and *Phobia* with text by John Vassos). The nine books extend over a momentous decade and their cumulative impact has escalated over the years.

The Vassos magnum opus is *Phobia.* Here he plunged deep into the unreal world of human fears, the distorture chambers of warped minds, portraying over a score of the insidious phantoms by which mortals are plagued. Vassos contends that a phobia is essentially graphic, the victim creating in his mind a realistic picture of that which he dreads.

Vassos' psychiatrist friend, Dr. Sullivan, who approved both the original outline and the final draft of *Phobia,* expressed amazement that a layman could have acquired such professional insight into clinical technicalities—but such is the acumen of Vassos. Dr. Abraham Brill, in reviewing the book, stated, "Remarkable how closely Vassos' illustrations delineate the true nature of phobias."

Gluck Sandor and Felicia Sorel, pioneering exponents of the modern dance, created a ballet around the phobia theme, the music by Lehman Engel. They interpreted its frenetic moods with terpsichorean sorcery, acting like possessed automatons.

In *Contempo* Vassos lashed out with an excoriating indictment of the crass exploitation and bamboozlement of various American enterprises.

In *Humanities* Vassos went all out in adroitly attacking the idiocy and futility of war, resulting in confusion and chaos, blind alleys and dead ends.

In *Ultimo* Vassos anticipated in the form of science fiction the current energy crisis and recent technological advances. The book deals with a fading sun, an ice age; people taking refuge underground, then swinging to the other extreme and seeking a new world, less cramped and closer to the sun; men in interstellar space, arriving on distant planets through magnetized tunnels in rockets, clothed in insulated garments and electrically oxygenated masks . . .

In *Kubla Khan*—the transcendent poem by Coleridge, the sublime somnambulist, written under the influence of opium—Vassos peered beyond the veil, depicted Coleridge's ethereal meandering between the finite and the infinite, aspiring to astral heights and Nirvana.

In *Elegy in a Country Church-Yard* Vassos' images have a wistful nostalgic tone that echoes variations of the theme line, "The paths of glory lead but to the grave." Dwelling on the lot of the common man, this meditative reverie pendulums between the fluctuations of existence: ambition and desire, fame and obscurity, resignation and hope.

Finally, we have the Wilde trilogy, where Vassos serves the reader with a sumptuous feast for the eye accompanied by considerable food for thought.

In *The Harlot's House* Vassos rhythmically collaborates with Wilde in composing visual decadence to match the erotic fantasy.

The Ballad of Reading Gaol, noted for its classic line "Each man kills the thing he loves," is a diapason of doom told by Vassos through barred shadows. The gaunt spectre of the gallows on a victim's soul is hauntingly depicted. The art critic C. J. Bulliet called the images in this book "so original and so brilliant that they constitute a mystical panorama of shapes and forms that parallel Wilde's verses instead of being merely their handmaiden or valet as is generally the case with book illustrations. Here is the first artist since Beardsley who has paralleled Wilde.''

In Vassos' version of *Salomé*—the macabre Wilde play, the production of which was halted by the pious Victorians—the heroine is a brazen vixen on the make as she lures John the Baptist into her labyrinthine toils, causing him to wind up by literally losing his head. The text pages of the original edition were showered with silvery stars, an added touch that befitted this historic lady of the evening.

As unusual as his art is the many-sided Vassos career. The Vassos family made its ancestral home in a small Greek village that bordered the Mediterranean. The seafaring folk of the community had as a backdrop lofty Mount Olympus.

Born in 1898, John inherited from his father his literary bent and from his mother, his artistic sensibilities. His early childhood was spent in Constantinople, where his father was the principal of a private school and editor of a Greek newspaper.

John recalls that, as a youngster, he had the innate inclination to draw. At the age of twelve, he was already motivated by liberal tendencies. For a few years he made political cartoons for a newspaper of radically different views from the one edited by his father. One of these cartoons poked fun at the Turkish senate. For a Greek, this was lèse-majesté. Immediately, there was a price on his head and hand. Even his father's influence could not intervene on his behalf. Before the young culprit could be apprehended, he had joined the crew of a British merchant vessel, as a deck hand—just before it weighed anchor.

This was the fateful year of 1914, and World War I had just broken out. Aboard this ship, Vassos had his first taste of adventure, as it cruised the seven seas picking up troops in China, India, Australia and the Far East.

In 1915, while serving on a British coaler operating in the North Sea, his ship was torpedoed. But he was saved from a watery grave only to tempt fate again—this time joining the British suicide fleet engaged in mine sweeping. After this, he participated in the ill-fated Gallipoli campaign with the British. He wound up in the American transport service, arriving in America in 1919, delivering a cargo of scrap iron to the port of Boston.

John's prime asset in his new country was an inherent confidence that he would make it with his art talent, and that the humblest job would be a stepping stone to his ultimate rise. He walked the streets until he stumbled on a job, that of window washer. Next he got a job lettering gaudy price tags and display cards for penny drugstore sales. His vivid effects evoked instant attention and stepped up sales. This crude response to his talent did much to reinforce his self-confidence.

From his meager earnings, John attended night classes at the Fenway Art School, where he had the opportunity to study under John Singer Sargent. Next we find young Vassos working as an assistant to Joseph Urban, the stage designer of Ziegfeld Follies fame. Business boomed for the Boston Opera Company with the joint productions of Urban and Vassos.

Next, John's roving quest for bigger and better opportunities for his burgeoning talent led him to the offices of Columbia Records. There he confidently told officials that he could do a lot more than they were doing in glamorizing the images of their artists. Vassos' exuberance got the green light and his presentations for such opera stars as Titta Ruffo, Maria Barrientos, Louis Graveure and a score of others added to the lustre and appeal of these famous names.

Now young Vassos decided it was time to test his talent in New York, establishing his own art studio, the New York Display Company, in mid-Manhattan. The year was 1924. John accepted anything and everything, upgrading whatever he did. Soon his name got around. At night he attended the Art Students League, where he had as instructors George Bridgman, John Sloan, Charles Hawthorne and Louis Bouché.

John's experience in working on stage sets in Boston came in handy when he got jobs to dress windows of such department stores as Namm's in Brooklyn and Macy's in Manhattan. Then his flair for dramatic showmanship secured commissions to execute spectacular murals for the lobbies of two Manhattan cinema palaces, the Rialto and the Rivoli. These highly pleased clients engaged John to do lobby displays for changing attractions, hypo-ing them with visual lures that caught passers-by.

This Broadway exposure of Vassos' originality won the attention of the publicity directors of leading department stores: Lord & Taylor, Bonwit Teller, Saks Fifth Avenue and Best & Co.

In a series of attention-commanding full-page advertisements, Vassos used the unique hard-line technique that he had been developing. This technique, which was to be featured in the various Vassos books, created a definite trend in graphics, which continues into the present.

Through the medium of black-and-white gouache (opaque watercolor) Vassos orchestrated fine gradations of light and shade. The utter simplicity of this method involved a severe discipline, for there was no recourse to easy air-brush effects.

The world of advertising, ever avid to connect with innovations, made further advances to Vassos. He was taken on his own terms and proceeded to produce advertisements for such distinguished accounts as Packard and the French Line which virtually stole the show wherever they appeared.

Vassos in 1933. Photo by Savero Antonelle.

Vassos in 1973. Photo by Douglas Fedor.

It was an easy transition to his new profession of industrial design, for he had already demonstrated a flair for harmonious contours. Then, as a back-up, he had a pragmatic philosophy of functionalism, of making things work. Added to this was a powerful drive to identity with the American scene on an everyday level. He met with considerable success in making objects easier to handle and to look at, blending good taste with good business. Vassos-designed objects included telephones, soft-drink dispensers, juke boxes, radio and television cabinets, turnstiles and fountain pens. A face-lotion bottle for Armand Products jumped sales 400%.

For some 42 years, Vassos was design consultant for RCA and was responsible for the organization of its design departments. In one year, his Magic Brain idea boosted RCA from fifth to first position in its field.

"Industrial design," he remarks, "took the curse off mass production, graced its products with personality and desirability."

Vassos' versatility is exercised by involvement in worthy causes that reward him by tapping his fertile potential. A tangent of this altruistic philosophy was responsible for launching him into the series of reputation-making books represented in this volume. This occurred when a Greek dramatic society asked him to design a souvenir program for the presentation of Wilde's *Salomé.* It marked the debut of Vassos' hard-line technique. The ravishing image of Salomé on the program cover (Plate 15 in this volume) created something of a sensation. It caught the eye of John Macrae, Jr., of E. P. Dutton. Without hesitation, he commissioned Vassos to do a book utilizing this technique. It proved an instant success.

A notable instance of Vassos' involvement occurred when he took hold of the Silvermine Guild of Artists in New Canaan. His broad-gauge policies and gift of leadership lifted this local art center into a nationally recognized institution. Its bold logo, designed by Vassos, consists of a tree with five branches, representing Painting, Sculpture, Drama, Music and Dance. One of the focal spots in the Guild complex is the Vassos Gallery, scene of many a memorable exhibition.

When World War II broke out, Vassos enlisted and was commissioned as a major in the intelligence service, from which he emerged with the rank of lieutenant colonel. His operations extended throughout the Middle East and North Africa. Among other things, he produced films and literature briefing military personnel on strategic tactics: how to break down codes and combat enemy propaganda and espionage.

Vassos has a conscientious sense of dedication to the nation of his adoption and to its democratic principles, which he feels pledged to defend against menaces that threaten to dilute and destroy values and loyalties.

However, Vassos views contemporary society with certain misgivings. Preoccupied with social problems, Vassos is disturbed by the coercions of mass media that deindividualize people into routine life styles. He is appalled by the stupidity and nonsense of these times— the gullibility of the public for specious values. Equally disturbing to Vassos is the cultural lag, as the juggernaut of science continues to make gigantic strides that dwarf other aspects of life.

Of a philosophical turn of mind, Vassos finds comfort in contemplating the fate of classic Hellenic art masterpieces. In his opinion, although they have undergone partial dismemberment by time and man, and have faced formidable odds, they have nevertheless survived because they personified a certain majesty, truth and beauty. Similarly, Vassos contends that those who stand firm in their ideas and ideals are destined to outlast their transient times.

Vassos decries the lack of style and manners in present-day society. He sees no quest for true elegance—the patina of culture—but finds with displeasure a contentment with two pompously elite and overworked concepts, "glamor" and "charisma." To him, these ideals are cheap and distasteful because they are too easily effected by means of slick tricks. This erudite cosmopolite feels there is an imperative need for the gracious consideration of niceties, refinements that will restore civilized amenities to our hectic way of life.

Now, in his mid-70's, there is still a bright glint in the Vassos eye that at once indicates an undiminished vitality of vision, since it has never ceased thriving on unique creative perceptions.

Contempo (1929): original frontispiece.

2. *Contempo* (1929): ''Advertising. An edifice reaching to the skies, and built on—BUNK.''

Contempo (1929): ''Electricity. One of the greater gods, all powerful and omnipresent.''

4. *Contempo* (1929): ''Prohibition. A vicious and obscene Bacchus has us in his power.''

Contempo (1929): ''The Market. Lashed by the whip of the tape.''

6. *Contempo* (1929): ''Commercialism. Chop down the forests. Harness men to desks.''

Contempo (1929): "Suburbia. Bridge. Bastard architecture. The large billboard of the develop-
ment company."

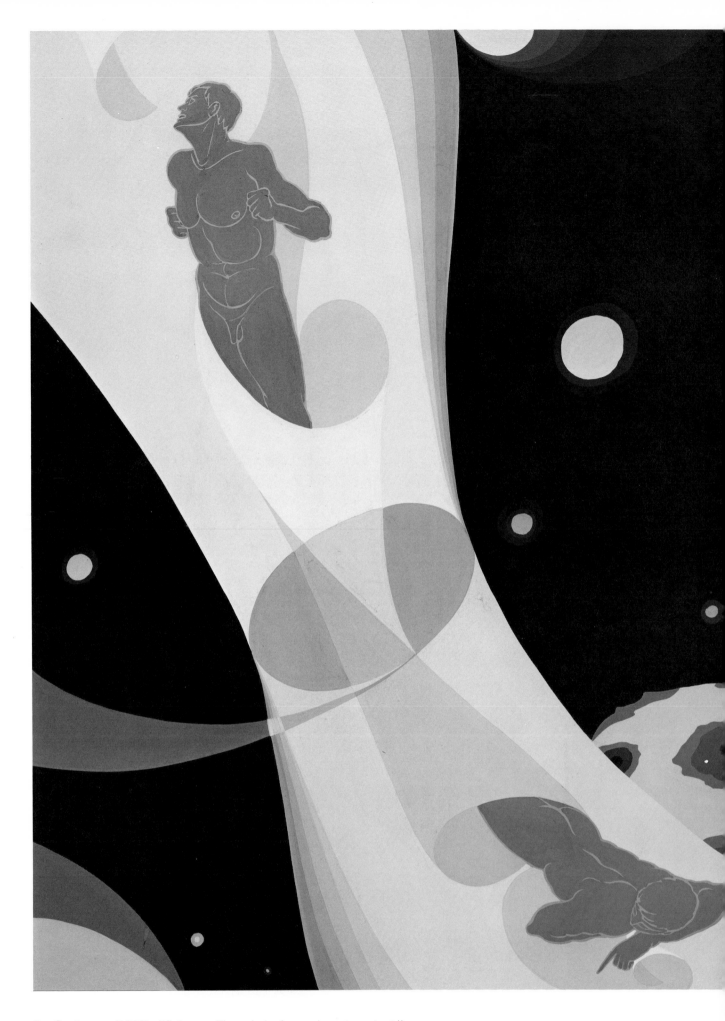

8. *Contempo* (1929): "Science. The mind of man is not content."

Salomé (1927): ''I am amorous of thy body, Jokanaan!''

10. *Salomé* (1927): The Death of the Young Syrian. [From the second edition.]

Salomé (1927): "I will dance for you, Tetrarch."

12. *Salomé:* The Dance of the Seven Veils. [Not in published book.]

13. *Salomé* (1927): ''The Executioner goes down into the cistern.''

14. *Salomé:* The Execution of Jokanaan. [Not in published book.]

5. *Salomé:* The Princess Receives Jokanaan's Head. [Earlier version (Nov. 1926) of the book illustration.]

16. *Salomé* (1927): ''I have kissed thy mouth, Jokanaan.''

7. *Salomé* (1927): "Death of Salomé."

18. *The Ballad of Reading Gaol* (1928): "Each man kills the thing he loves."

The Ballad of Reading Gaol (1928): "I never saw a man who looked So wistfully at the day."

20. *The Ballad of Reading Gaol* (1928): ''And drank the morning air.''

The Ballad of Reading Gaol (1928): ''Gaped for a living thing.''

22. *The Ballad of Reading Gaol* (1928): ''Horror stalked before each man, And Terror crept behind.''

23. *The Ballad of Reading Gaol:* endpaper design not used in book (the feeling of imprisonment).

34. The Billard at Banville Cook embosses design not used in book (freedom; destruction of the

The Harlot's House (1929): ''The Harlot's House.'' Portrait of Wilde at lower left.

26. *The Harlot's House* (1929): ''E Tenebris.''

The Harlot's House (1929): "On the Recent Sale by Auction of Keats' Love Letters."

28. *Ultimo* (1930): original frontispiece.

Ultimo (1930): "Caught in the ice of the North Atlantic the last great liner called for help."

30. *Ultimo* (1930): "All touch between far distant cities was lost."

1. *Ultimo* (1930): ''Into the frozen earth bored the huge electric drills.''

32. *Ultimo* (1930): "A great carrion bird would sweep down from the air."

Ultimo (1930): "Tube delivery [of food] is almost instantaneous."

34. *Ultimo* (1930): An Underground Population Center.

5. *Ultimo* (1930): "Sub-ocean expeditions are in vogue of late."

36. *Ultimo* (1930): ''The ever weakening crimson rays of the dying sun gleam on the chasmed earth.''

Ultimo (1930): ''In deep caverns far within the bowels of the earth.''

38. *Ultimo* (1930): ''Alter the course of this earth that we may approach very much nearer the sun.''

39. *Ultimo* (1930): ''We cast from us the shell of an earth now useless and dead.''

40. *Gray's Elegy* (1931): "Can honour's voice provoke the silent dust?"

1. *Gray's Elegy* (1931): "Some heart once pregnant with celestial fire."

42. *Gray's Elegy* (1931): "Some mute inglorious Milton here may rest."

3. *Gray's Elegy* (1931): "Far from the madding crowd's ignoble strife."

44. *Gray's Elegy* (1931): "And many a holy text around she strews."

Gray's Elegy (1931): ''E'en from the tomb the voice of nature cries.''

46. *Gray's Elegy* (1931): ''Slow through the church-way path we saw him borne.''

Gray's Elegy (1931): "A youth, to fortune and to fame unknown."

48. *Gray's Elegy* (1931): ''The bosom of his Father and his God.''

Phobia (1931): original frontispiece. Man emerges from an artificial womb.

50. *Phobia* (1931): "Nyctophobia, the Fear of the Dark."

. *Phobia* (1931): ''Astrophobia, the Fear of Storms.''

52. *Phobia* (1931): "Zoophobia, the Fear of Animals."

8. *Phobia* (1931): "Potamophobia, the Fear of Running Water."

54. *Phobia* (1931): "Hylophobia, the Fear of the Forest."

5. *Phobia* (1931): "Necrophobia, the Fear of the Dead."

56. *Phobia* (1931): "Acrophobia, the Fear of High Places."

7. *Phobia* (1931): "Climacophobia, the Fear of Falling Down Stairs."

58. *Phobia* (1931): ''Batophobia, the Fear of Falling Objects [and Passing by High Buildings].''

9. *Phobia* (1931): "Dromophobia, the Fear of Crossing the Street."

60. *Phobia* (1931): "Aichmophobia, the Fear of Sharp and Pointed Objects."

51. *Phobia* (1931): "Agrophobia, the Fear of Open Spaces."

62. *Phobia* (1931): "Claustrophobia, the Fear of Enclosed Spaces."

3. *Phobia* (1931): ''Monophobia, the Fear of Being Alone.''

64. *Phobia* (1931): ''Topophobia, the Fear of Situations—Stagefright.''

. *Phobia* (1931): ''Kleptophobia, the Fear of Stealing.''

66. *Phobia* (1931): "Mysophobia, the Fear of Dirt and Contamination."

Phobia (1931): "Anthropophobia, the Fear of People."

68. *Phobia* (1931): "Phagophobia, the Fear of Swallowing."

9. *Phobia* (1931): "Syphilophobia, the Fear of Syphilis."

70. *Phobia* (1931): "Hypnophobia, the Fear of Sleep."

1. *Phobia* (1931): ''Pantophobia, the Fear of Everything.''

72. *Kubla Khan* (1933): "In Xanadu."

3. *Kubla Khan* (1933): ''Where Alph, the sacred river, ran.''

74. *Kubla Khan* (1933): "And here were gardens bright with sinuous rills."

5. *Kubla Khan* (1933): ''A mighty fountain momently was forced.''

76. *Kubla Khan* (1933): ''Huge fragments vaulted like rebounding hail.''

7. *Kubla Khan* (1933): ''Ancentral voices prophesying war!''

78. *Kubla Khan* (1933): ''A sunny pleasure-dome with caves of ice!''

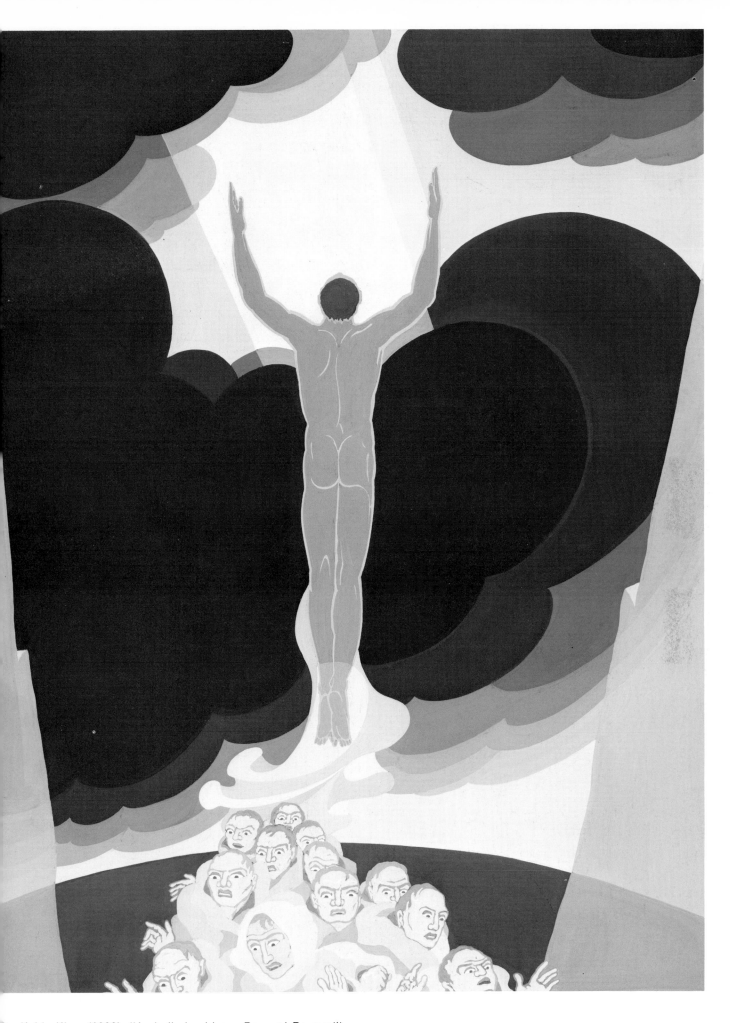

9. *Kubla Khan* (1933): ''And all should cry, Beware! Beware!''

80. *Humanities* (1935): "Peace. We shall march to victory over the graves of our fallen comrades."

81. *Humanities* (1935): ''Education. Open your mouths, boys— There, wasn't that good!''

82. *Humanities* (1935): "Disarmament. The race is on."

83. *Humanities* (1935): "Food. Starvation exists in the midst of plenty."

84. *Humanities* (1935): "Frontiers. Build the walls high and thick."

85. *Humanities* (1935): "Science. Finding ways to slaughter millions."

86. *Humanities* (1935): ''Philanthropy. Let the university be named after the tobacco king.''

87. *Humanities* (1935): "The Machine. It has released us from the slavery of toil."

88. *Humanities* (1935): ''Emancipation. Free in name only.''

89. *Humanities* (1935): ''Enlightenment. Freedom of the Press. Is it freedom to distort facts?''

90. *Humanities* (1935): "The Church. The promise of happiness in the hereafter."

91. *Humanities* (1935): ''Homo Sapiens. Quantity production of human beings.''

92. *Humanities* (1935): "Sovereignty. After the explorer—the soldier."

93. *Humanities* (1935): "Nationalism. By patriotism out of imperialism is born nationalism."

94. *Humanities* (1935): "The Old. The never-ending sacrifice of youth to age."

95. *Humanities* (1935): "The Workers. Property must be protected—the worker is an enemy."

96. *Humanities* (1935): "Justice. One law for the rich, another for the poor."

97. *Humanities* (1935): "Individualism. The right to amass huge sums of money."

98. *Humanities* (1935): "Child Labor. Little bodies are cheap."

99. *Humanities* (1935): ''The Critics. Pellets of wisdom in the gaping mouths of the hungry public.''

100. *Humanities* (1935): "Ethics. Fealty to the fellow members of his profession."

101. *Humanities* (1935): ''The Leaders. Innumerable prophets ready to lead us.''

102. ''Okhi'' (1939): the Greek word for ''no,'' the nation's reply to the invading Fascists; one of Vassos' few posters.

03. "The Abduction of Helen of Troy" (1935): magazine illustration.

104. Magazine illustration (1931).

105. Unpublished design for a magazine illustration (1931): man returning to a devastated land.

106. ''Tango Tragico'' (1935): magazine illustration.

107. ''The Island of the Dead'': unpublished design for a magazine illustration.

109. Design for a "Ballet Mécanique" in the unproduced Billy Rose show of 1926.

110. Magazine illustration (1931) for a story by Aldous Huxley about super-ants taking over the earth.

111. Study for a General Tires ad campaign (1924).

112. Ad for the Cammeyer shoe salon.

113. Ad for the Cammeyer shoe salon.

ARISTOCRAT OF THE METROPOLIS

THE Packard Stationary Coupe is much favored by professional men. This new Aristocrat of the Metropolis—available both on the Packard Eight and Eight De Luxe Chassis—embodies distinction and luxury sincerely appreciated by men whose pursuits call them constantly about the city. Men and women whose activities are business or social also find it a most convenient personal car, both in town and country. A comfortable rumble seat permits extra passengers—large and accessible compartments accommodate belongings. ¶ May we demonstrate the aristocratic Packard Stationary Coupe? May we show you how its *Ride Control* provides a degree of riding comfort that exists in no other make of motor vehicle?

ASK THE MAN WHO OWNS ONE

VAS905

PACKARD

PACKARD MOTOR CAR COMPANY OF NEW YORK

Eleventh Avenue at 54th Street   Broadway at 61st Street   Broadway at Sherman Avenue

BRONX: 696 East Fordham Road   BROOKLYN: Atlantic at Classon Avenue

PARK AVENUE PACKARD, Inc.   WEST END PACKARD CO., Inc.

6 East 57th Street   Broadway at 106th Street

114. Ad for the Packard car.

115. Ad for a Bonwit Teller perfume.